TELL ME ABOUT YOURSELF

Max Popov

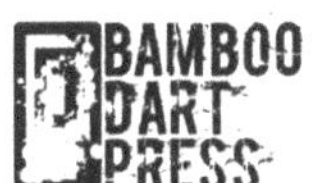

LOS ANGELES † NEW YORK † LONDON † MELBOURNE

Tell Me About Yourself by Max Popov

ISBN: 978-1-947240-76-6 Paperback

ISBN: 978-1-947240-77-3 eBook

First Printing 2023

Cover art by Max Popov

Layout and design by Mark Givens

For information:

Bamboo Dart Press

chapbooks@bamboodartpress.com

Bamboo Dart Press 036

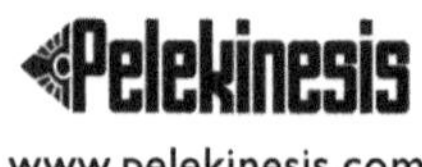

www.pelekinesis.com

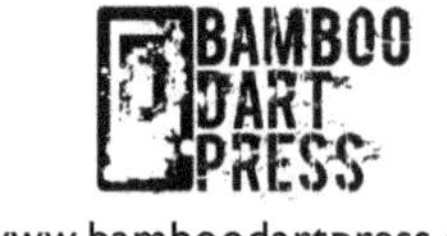

www.bamboodartpress.com

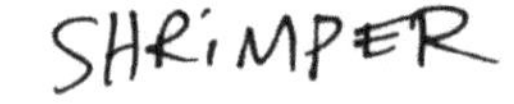

www.shrimperrecords.com

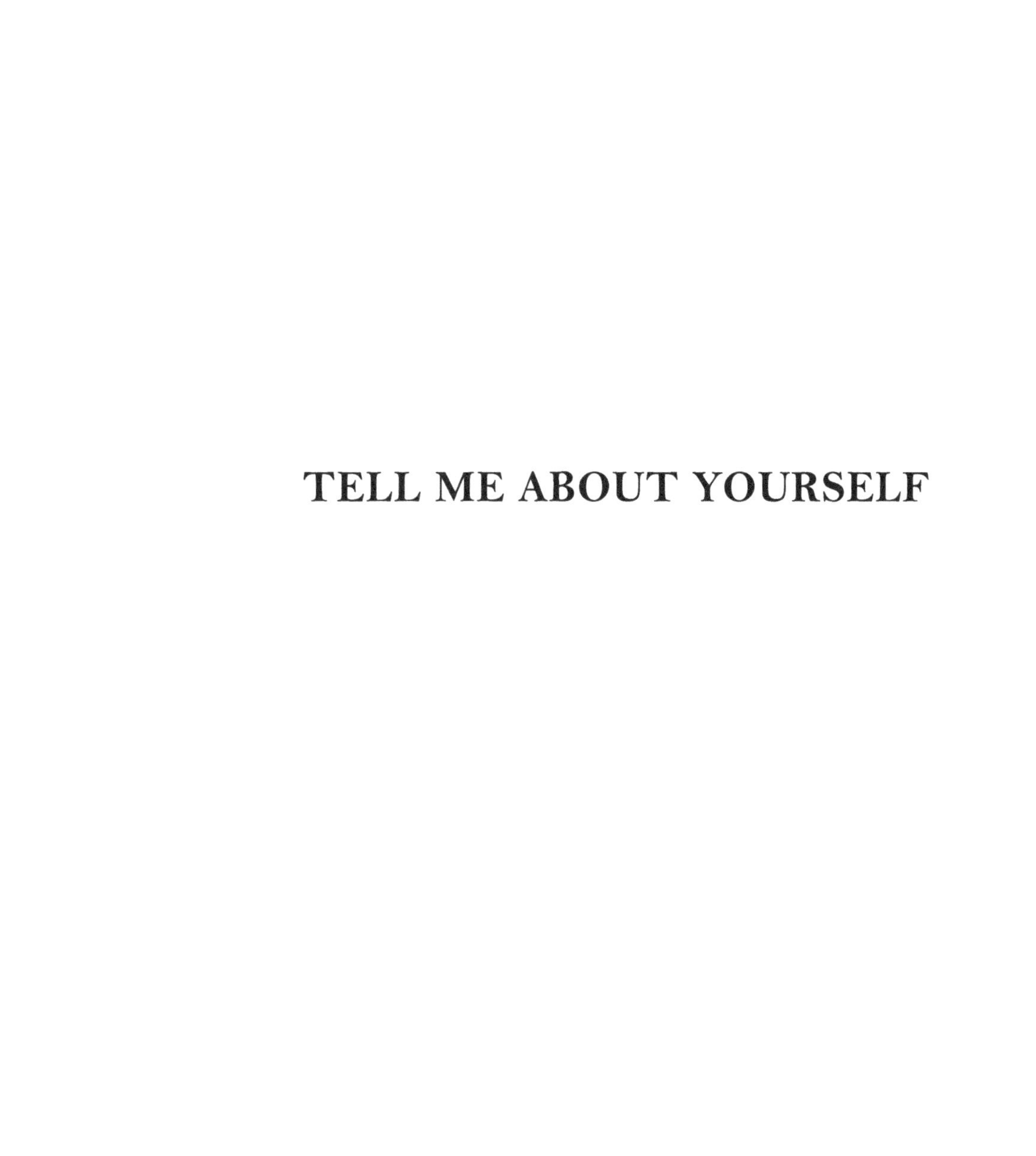

TELL ME ABOUT YOURSELF

Over the course of 1975 and much of 1976, the period of my adulthood when I was most afflicted by childish nightmares, from early evening until the middle of the night—to put off going to sleep, I suppose—I asked neighbors I'd chitchatted with in my tenement building ("The Alpine," a seven-story walk up at 125 Second Avenue, where I lived in a sunny but bleak apartment on the top floor in the back) as well as strangers at B & H Dairy (the hole-in-the-wall diner in the building next door), Gem Spa (the newsstand on the corner), and a bar (the name of which I forget, across the street), if I could make a drawing of them naked.

All but a few didn't even blink an eye. They wanted to be assured, though, that they would be portrayed with an air of dignity. *That* was the stumbling block. I always disclosed that my drawing skills were poor, perhaps even, as many had said—and I was the last person on earth to disagree—pathetic. Even I realized, I told them, that my drawings looked like the toilet graffiti on the stalls of men's public bathrooms.

Nevertheless, a few people accepted my invitation, perhaps out of vanity or pity or boredom, who's to say what motivated them. Here are my drawings of them and also their tape-recorded responses to my request "Tell me about yourself," made to my fellow tenants in their apartments while they posed, to the others, in the local haunts before they came all the way up to my apartment to pose.

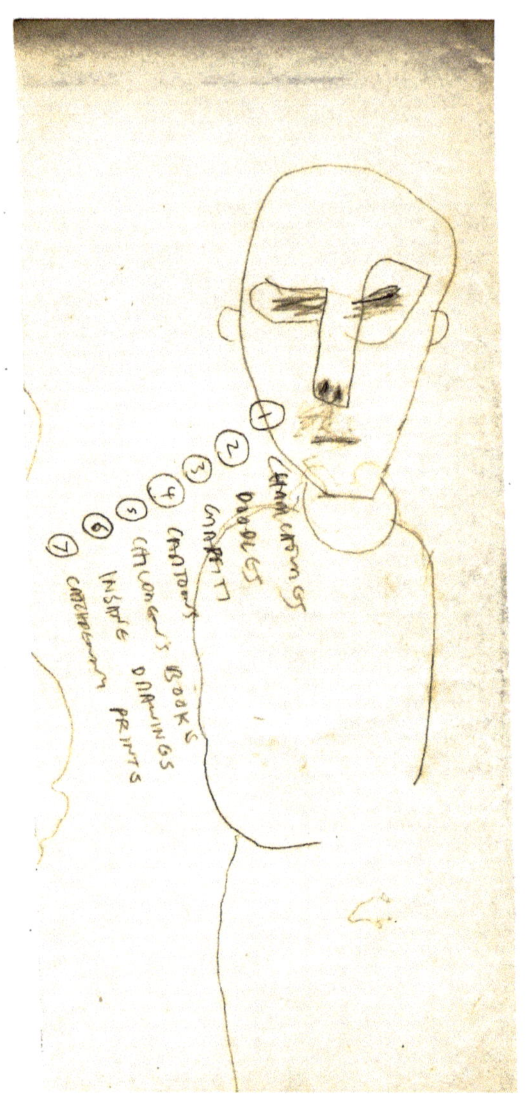
2 DOODLES
3 GRAFFITI
4 CARTOONS
5 CHILDREN'S BOOKS
6 INSIDE DRAWINGS
PRINTS

About a year ago I had a nervous breakdown. It was due to "distressing life scenarios." Never mind what. I'd have to know you better to tell you. All you have to know is that since then I've wised up. I used to be dutiful, congenial, and cautious. Now I let the maggots eat the cat food. No matter the season or location, outside or inside, irregardless, I wear a wide-brim sun hat. I "disturb the peace in public areas." I visit prostitutes. (Don't misunderstand. Just to chat with them. They get lonely, too, you know.) Where is my hat? I need to put my hat back on immediately.

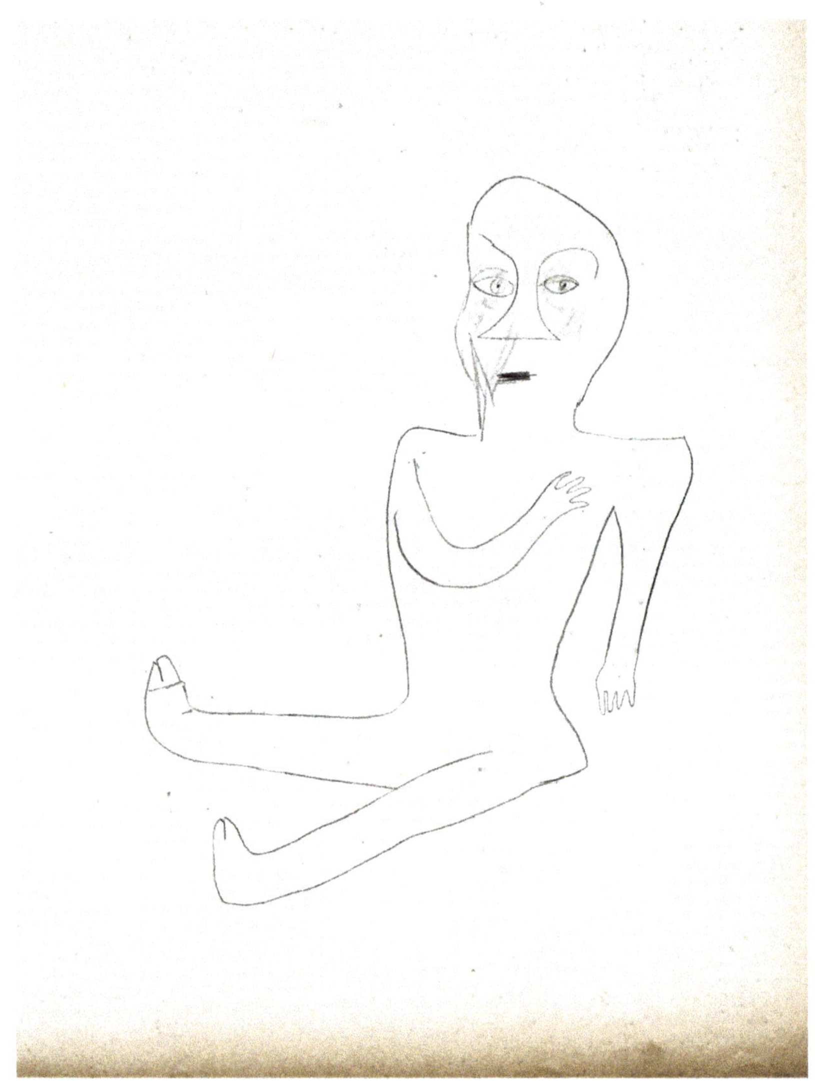

To be looked straight in the eye is offensive to me. It's just this kind of forced intimacy that betrays a man's insincerity. It's a trick of queers and salesmen. Unless it's merely a poor sense of rhythm, you know what I mean. Because sometimes even people intimate with each other don't realize that if you're going to slip into the intervals between snapshots, then you need time to avert your eyes, to look about, to hesitate, even to fumble a little and look down.

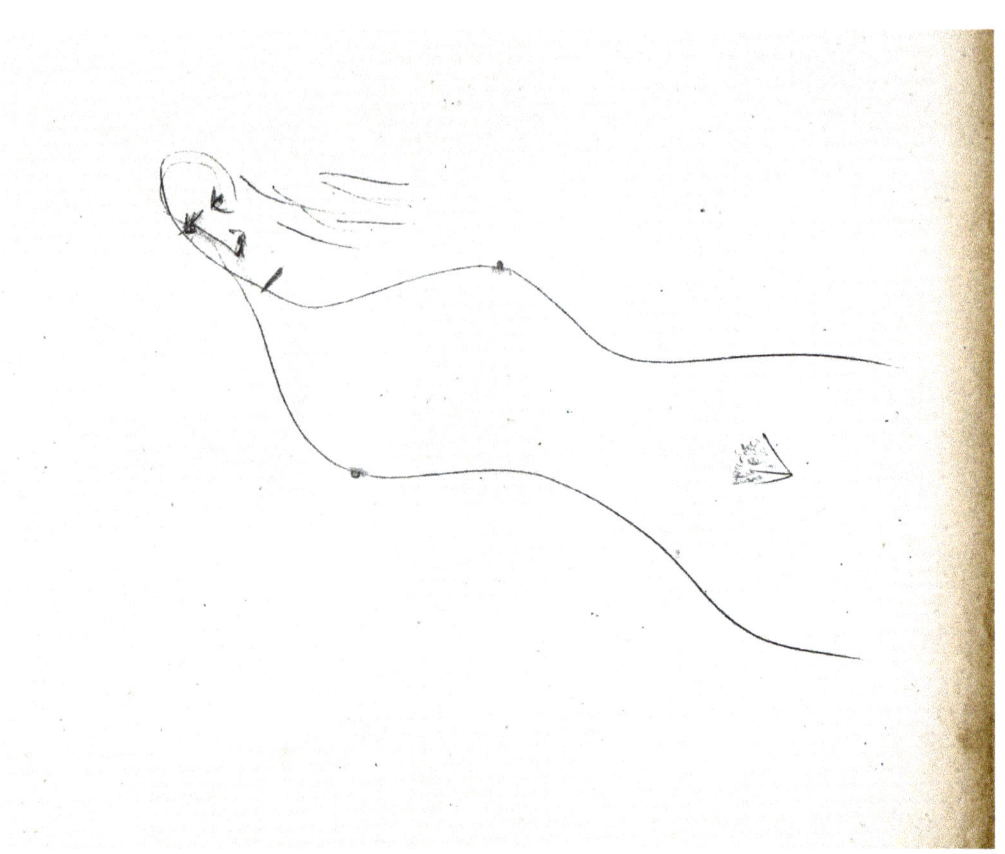

Agh! I feel like such a rucksack. I carry everywhere and I carry heavy. And for what? Just to have certain people shove me aside and poke me. Well, I don't like it. I'm not a major obstacle. In fact, I'm no obstacle at all. Just because I don't have anything to do with people except in superficial ways (which I recognize very well, thank you) doesn't mean I don't have feelings. Certain people already know this.

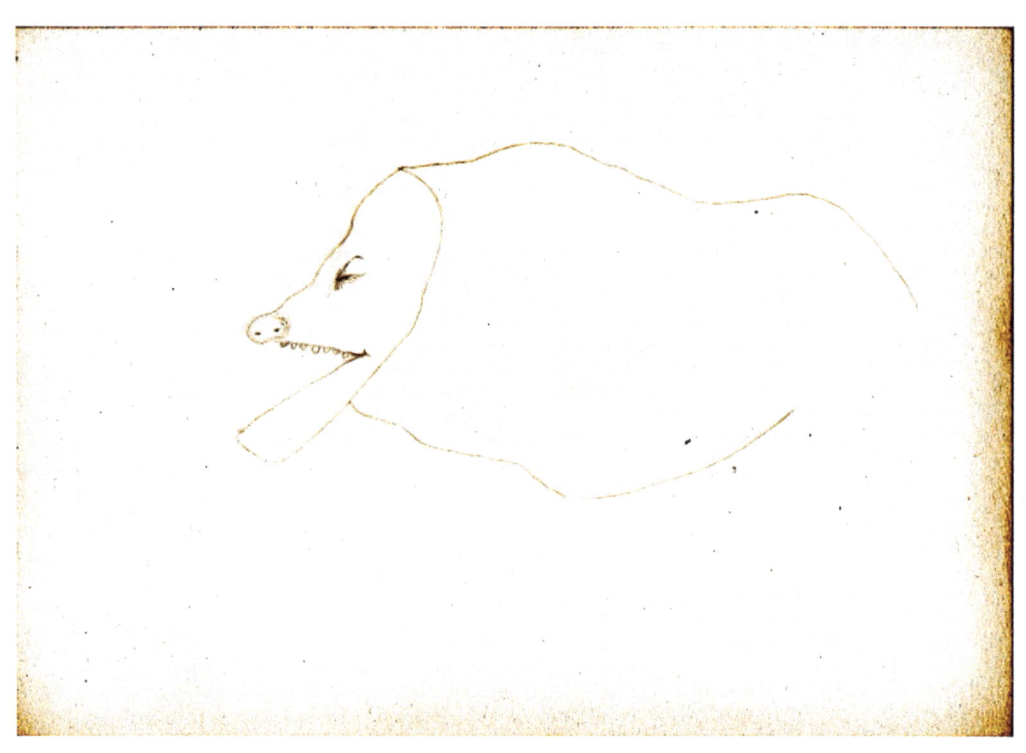

I eat mud radishes. I'm actually about to chomp one down with my borscht. (Let me just…rummage around a bit… in my bag here…) Mind you, it won't be my only one of the day. Not by any means. It's said that their sulfur content promotes bile flow. But I've been eating them ever since I found out they're good for producing certitude. Sometimes they back up on me. But I'm used to the belch of cocksureness. Don't forget, I've been teaching twenty years. In my line of business, we provide a top-notch service and get the best results. The taxpayers demand it. In my personal opinion, we're all part of the system. Ah! Here's one!

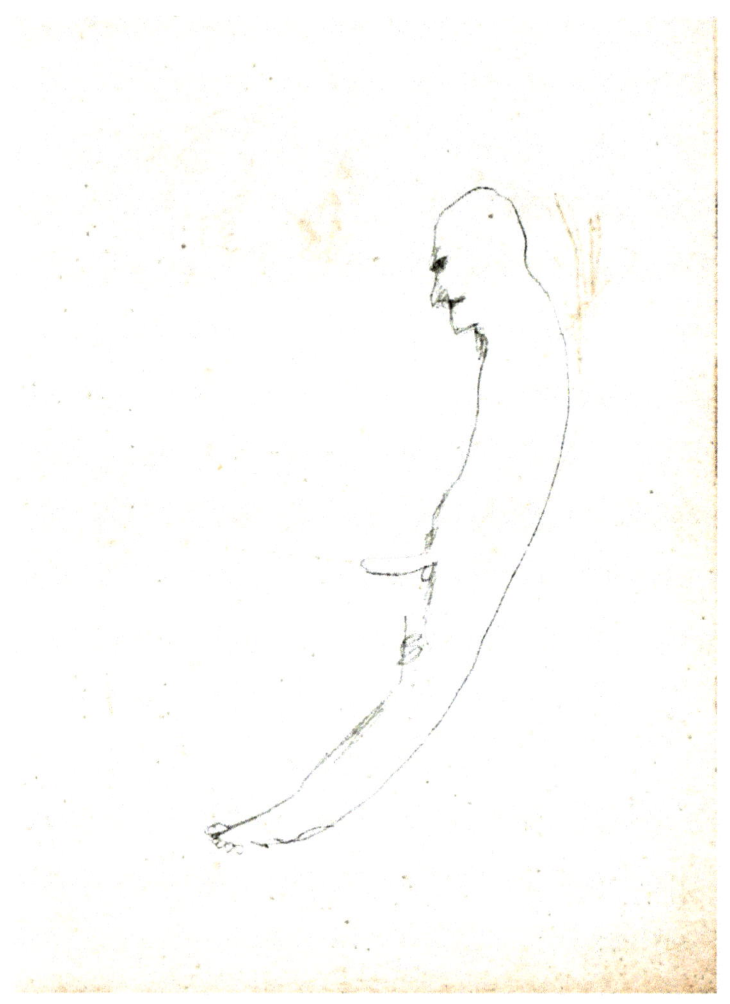

It's not logical, I know, to believe that I'll be deceived again, no more than it's strictly logical to assume that the sun will rise tomorrow just because it always has. Yet how could we even take a step if we didn't assume some natural order? I used to think that all I had to do is "look inside myself," as they say, to find out why I was being deceived. But after two marriages and a few affairs, I realized that the mere wheeze from my throat is intimately related to the rattle of leaves. So I gave up all hope of love and happiness. God knows where I got those notions from anyway. Oh, if there was only one woman who could possibly understand.

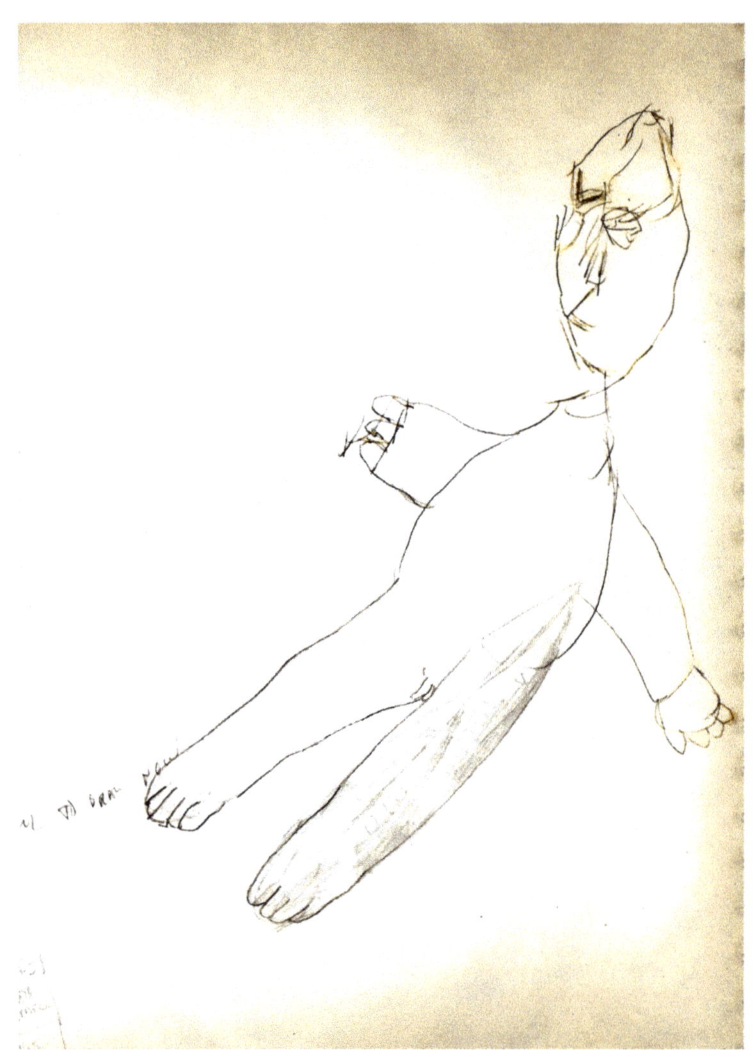

I'm not a well man. My head is like a plant, of which great things were once expected, but which has now begun to grow mold. My hands and feet are like crayfish fresh out of the red swamp, crawling over dry land. The innards of my stomach are like the remains of a dead fowl. I've been sleeping so much that dreaming has replaced watching movies. (Look over there. See? I keep a bag of popcorn and a box of Raisinets on the night table.) But all this time lying down has enabled me to locate my exact center, the place where you could twirl me about, if you had a mind to. Would you like to give it a try?

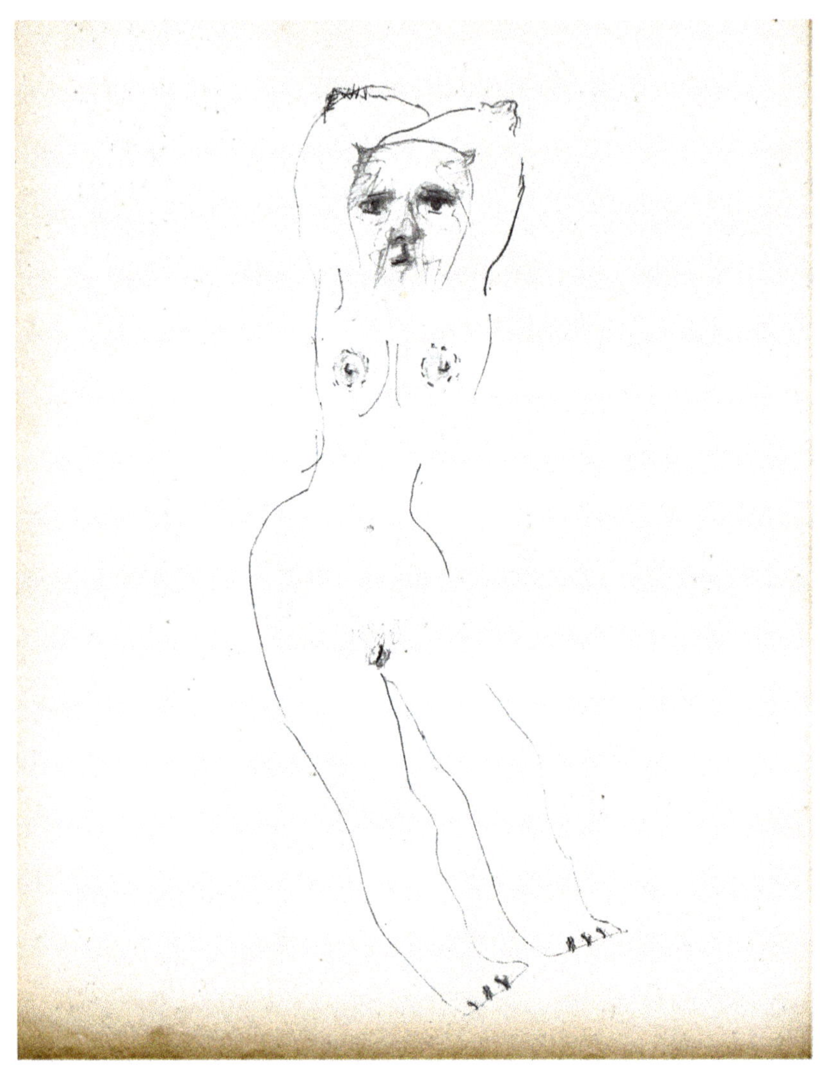

I ask myself if I've grown older on my own strengths or on the weaknesses of others. I can never tell whether I'm being appreciated or merely being tolerated by my staff or even by my own children. I admit that it might appear that I'm devious and contrary. But I take it for granted everything will come out even, so I never steal and I never give to charity. Still, I never know how much of the pain of others is my fault and how much is the way things are supposed to be. I guess you'd have to say I'm working on faith because there are so many things I don't understand.

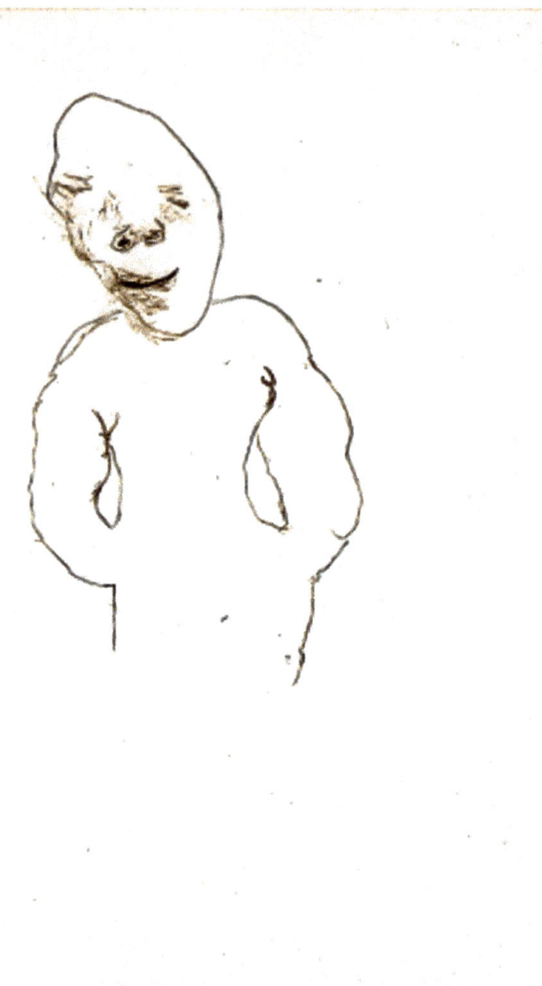

There are a few things that I want to tell you. That I'm an architect. I mainly design very cool parking garages with cars haphazardly piled on top of each other like in a junkyard. That in my set I'm considered to be rich and successful. That here I'm just another schlimazel having drinks. (Come closer. This bar was my father's hangout. He disappeared when I was ten. My mother said he was taken for a ride, a Murder, Inc. thing. I come down here once a month because I think he might show up. Move back.) That I've always followed the rules, in both my professional and personal life. That I'm secretly seeking a dispensation. Don't I deserve one?

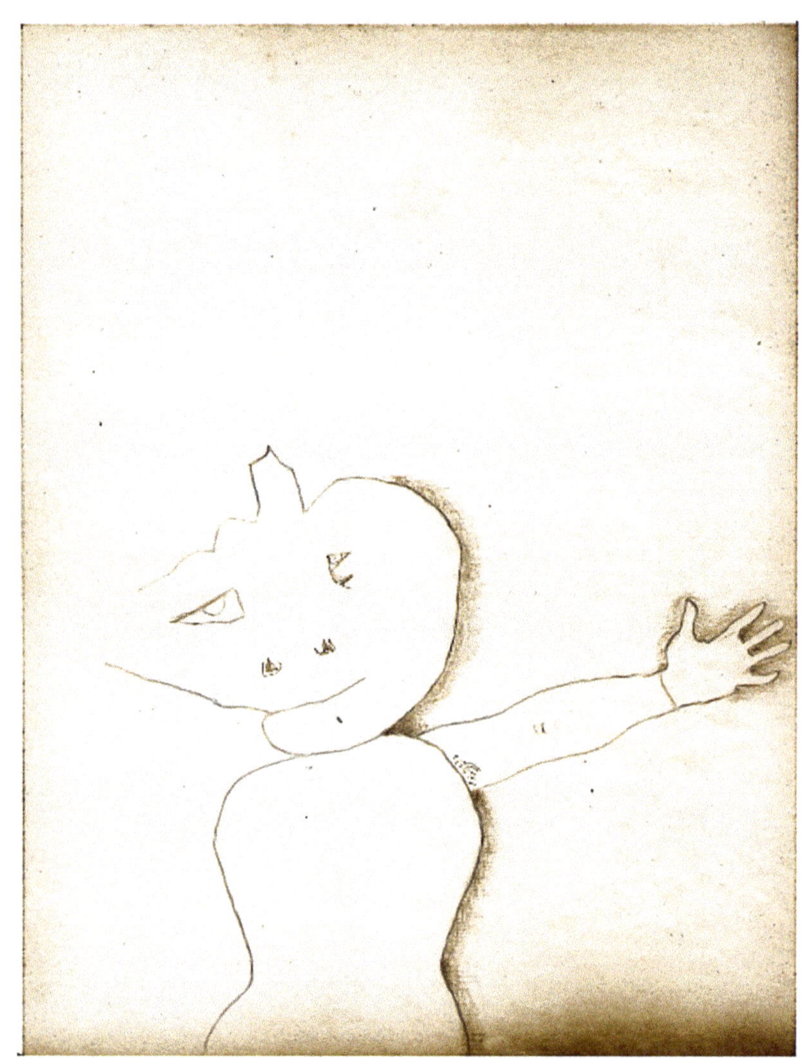

I can't stand my wife. She always has a cold. She uses a crumpled handkerchief, which she keeps stuffed up her sleeve, to snatch her sneezes at the nostrils before they can get out into the world where they'll misbehave. I tell her, "Stop it. Stop being sickly." But that only seems to make her nose redder and her eyes more watery. For years I told her that I was going to leave her for a plump, rosy-cheeked woman. But one day she said, "Well, go ahead, if you're so impatient." At that moment I realized that without me she'd die. So what can I do? I'm stuck with her.

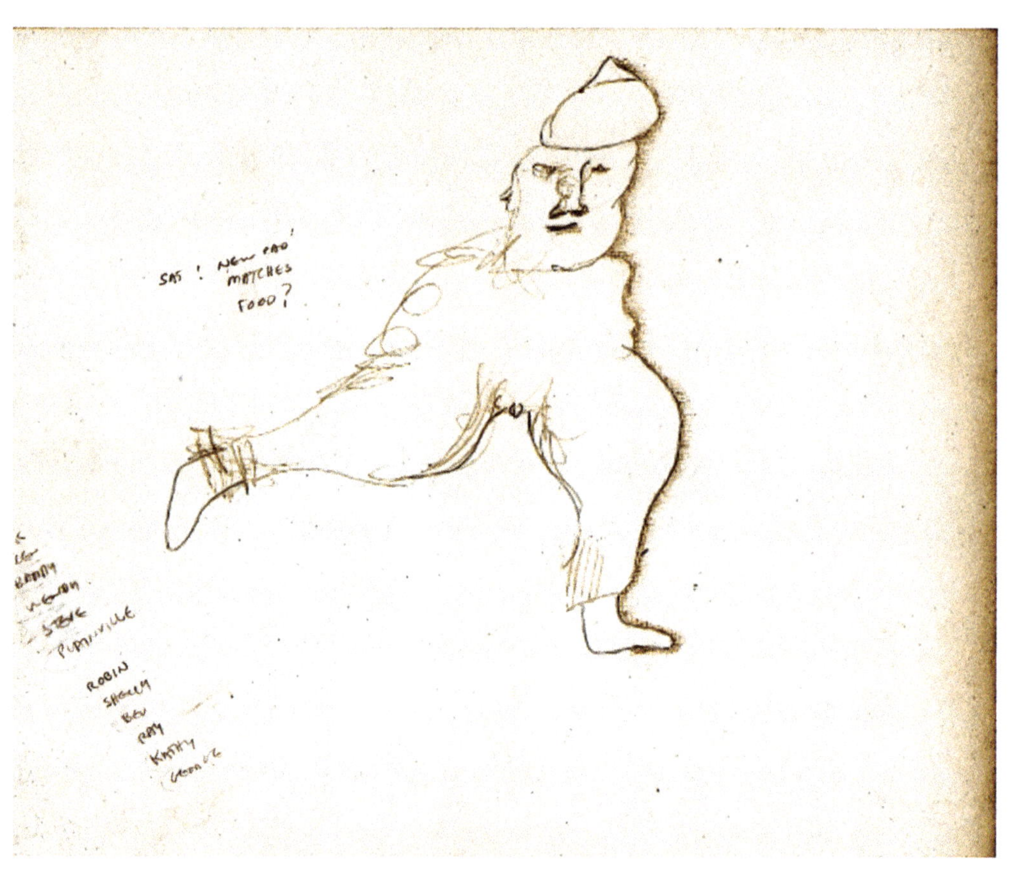
SAT ! NEW PAD !
MATCHES
FOOD ?
STEVE
ROBIN
BEV
RAY
KATHY

My mother (poor Mommy, I wish I had been kinder to you!) always told me it was good to get out of the apartment. Of course, that's easier said than done. Not that I never get out. In fact, recently I've been walking around a lot late at night. Yes, it can be dangerous. Believe me, I know. A couple of weeks ago in the Alphabets I was beaten up by this no-neck pinhead who cried afterward and begged me to forgive him. I told him I honestly didn't have the time. Funny I've never bumped into you, what with I stop off here every Wednesday to pick up *The Voice*, and you say you live just a few doors down. I think that's because I always hurry along, minding my own business.

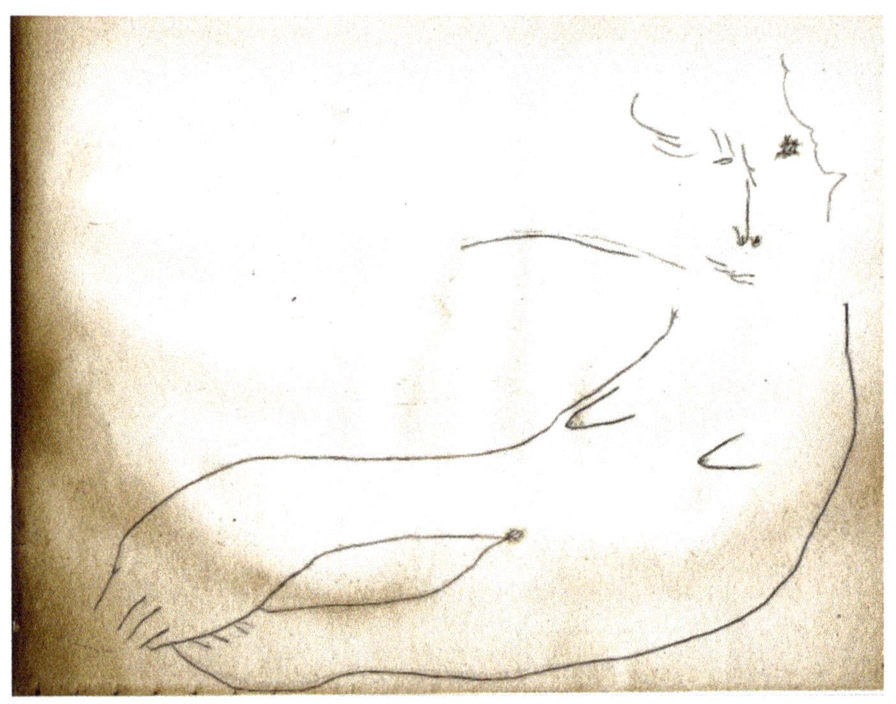

Everybody's been telling me to live a little. I tell them you've got to be careful, that even a little excitement might cause nervous exhaustion. What's there to get excited about anyway? Dancing? My feet are so swollen I can hardly stand up. There's no more doin' the hanky panky for me. (You put your big toe in. You pull your big toe out. You put your big toe in. And you shake it all about.) My footloose and fanny-free days are over. I don't know much about excitement, but I'm sure it's pretty awful to the touch. Cheers!

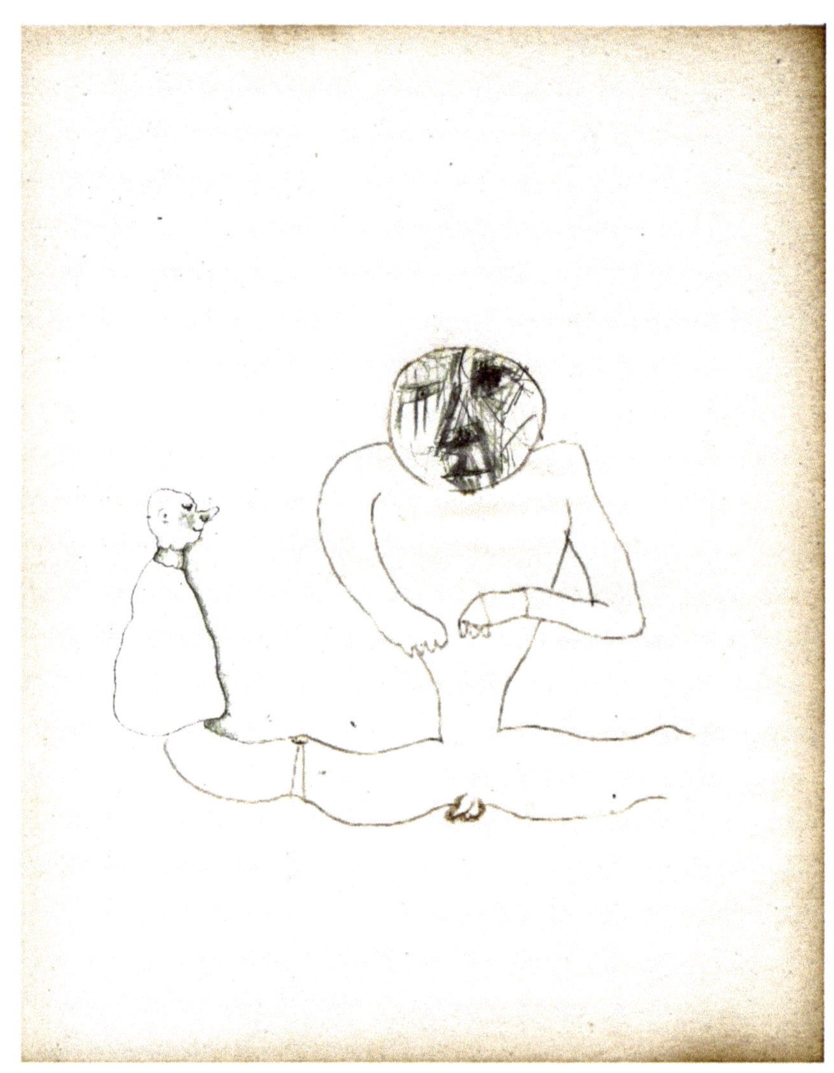

I and those neighbors who took part in my unusual—some might say, bizarre—project happily lived like immigrants in that tenement building on Second Avenue. We boasted about having our tub in the kitchen (I often—my heart flutters upon recalling it!—plunked my feet in the sink). But I felt little connection to them, despite this commonality, or to the participants who lived elsewhere, even after they posed naked and told me about themselves. I just couldn't fathom the lives they led, a failing I attributed to my being younger than them.

Now I'm far older than they were then. Only to find myself no more able to fathom my own life than I could theirs. And when looking at this recent self-portrait, I even ask, "Is that me here, the weary old man, or over there, the sly trickster?" For that matter, who is this me who must persist? Doesn't somebody else need my current apartment? If only I might find a face in my mirror when, upon waking in the middle of the night, under my breath I whisper, "Is anybody here?"

Acknowledgments

My friend Bob Hirschfeld, who died ten years ago, inhabits the pages of *Tell Me About Yourself* like a spirit. In the mid-1970s we wrote responses to the eponymous request made to the characters that I'd drawn. This rudimentary version of the text languished for about the next 35 years. In 2011 I began making a number of significant changes, additions, and deletions needed to fully develop the text. Many mischievous, soulful character utterances created by Bob are embedded in the final version. It's in them where he is present.

Thanks to my co-publisher Mark Givens, who not only guided the manuscript to publication but also created an elegant layout and design for the cover and, through his wizardry, produced scans that captured the vibrancy of the original drawings, now faded; fellow Bamboo Dart Press author Peter Wortsman, who forthwith recommended the manuscript to Mark; and, most of all, my guardian angel Susan Landry, who not only helped me find a small press home for *Tell Me About Yourself* by sending the manuscript to Peter but also championed my creation of this screwy little book to me.

About the Author

Max Popov is a writer and yoga teacher.

He is the author of *The Tempest: The Graphic Novel*; *Weight-Resistance Yoga: Practicing Embodied Spirituality*; *The Path of Modern Yoga: The History of an Embodied Spiritual Practice* (published under the name Elliott Goldberg); and two entries in *Yoga: L' encyclopédie*: "Yogendra et Kuvalayananda: santé et bien-être pour tous par le yoga" [Yogendra and Kuvalayananda: health and well-being for all through yoga"] and "L'invention de la salutation au Soleil" ["The creation of the sun salutations"] (published under the name Elliott Goldberg).

He teaches, in-person and remotely, suspended-body yoga, a regime for performing exercises that systematically strengthen and stretch all the major muscles using a suspension training device (a long inelastic strap anchored to the top of a door) as an at-home yogic movement meditation practice.

To read Popov's reflections on *Tell Me About Yourself*, learn more about his other published works, and find out about his yogic strength and flexibility training, you can view his web page at maxpopovwriteryogateacher.com.

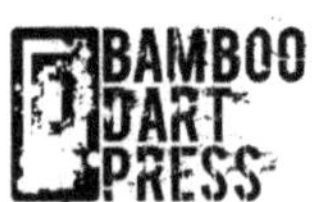

112 N. Harvard Ave. #65
Claremont, CA 91711

chapbooks@bamboodartpress.com

www.bamboodartpress.com